LIFI
OLD FOLKS HOME
WHERE THE ELDERLY GO TO DIE

DOUGLAS RICHIE

outskirts
press

To my son Teddy, for the countless hours he devoted to editing my manuscript. It is a better piece of work because of his efforts.

Table of Contents

Author's Notes

As the years roll by, I find that the activities I can participate in are reduced. Living without my beloved Annie has
required many adjustments. No more cruises. No more
dancing. Life's little pleasures are now reduced to playing
bridge, enjoying a good meal, reading, and writing. By writing I mean that which results in the self-publishing of a book.

My life's big pleasure is without a doubt, having a visit from
one or more members of my extended family

Once I was turned on to the work of David McCullough,
the highly regarded American historian, I stopped reading
Vince Flynn and his ilk. On days when I spend my idle hours
reading, there is no sense of accomplishment. Contrarily,
if the time is spent writing a new book, I go to the dining
room with an appetite and a sense of accomplishment.

I have depended on my uncanny memory to provide the
material for the four books that I have written. I do not
write fiction. At least not intentionally. I believe everything
I have written is based on fact. I have not kept a diary or a

journal. I depend on my memory for the material that produces my books.

Several residents who are aware that I am an author, have asked what my next book will be about. When I tell them I have stopped writing, I receive encouragement to begin a new book.

Someone suggested that I write about our experiences living in a retirement community. There must be a wealth material on this subject.

So, here we are.

Preface

For 23 years we had been the owner/operators of a 28-unit hotel called Warm Sands Villa, in the heart of Palm Springs, California. Our primary home was in a three story, 13-unit apartment building which we named Lido Sands. It was located right on the beach of Alamitos Bay in Long Beach, California.

Throughout those 23 years we commuted nearly every week between Long Beach and Palm Springs. I felt as though I could drive those 111 miles blind-folded.

Should the reader have any interest in learning what it is like to be an owner/manager of a motel, I refer you to my book, *Entrepreneurial Annie and I.*

Our investment in Maui did not require any of our time or effort as it was handled for us by a very competent management company. Our only management responsibility was Lido Sands where we lived full time.

The next twelve years were devoted to several fun activities.

We were making up for those 23 years of intensely hard work.

We went to a lot of movies. We tried new restaurants. We took dancing lessons at a senior center. We flew to Philadelphia every year to visit Annie's parents and her sister Joan with her large family. We took a lot of cruises.

Description of a CCRC

A CCRC enables the resident to live independently if he/she is able. An assisted living department is available for residents who are ambulatory but require help with personal care. The skilled nursing department serves the needs of residents who are recovering from surgery or a long term-illness.

Independent living in a well-managed and economically sound CCRC offers the choice of several floor plans, ranging from a small studio to a large two bedroom with two bathrooms. Each includes a fully equipped kitchen.

A private bedroom with bath is provided for residents in the assisted-living department. A separate dining room dedicated to the assisted living residents is provided.

Based on my experience at CBTS, the assisted living department also has several nurses who respond to a problem with a resident such as a fall. Some of these people are LVNs but most of them are CNA's. A service can be purchased that will deliver prescribed medications. Prescriptions will be renewed as need.

I speak from experience, having been a patient in the Care Center several times, regarding the high quality of service and care that is provided by our skilled nursing department. Its reputation is such that hospitals throughout north San Diego County refer their patients who need follow up care from surgery or illness, to CBTS.

Patients in the skilled nursing department have the option of private or semi-private room. Each has a bath within the room. Medications and meals are brought to the patient. Physical therapists and occupational therapists work within the department. Patients are encouraged to utilize their ability. Attention is given to making the patient comfortable by keeping their bed clean and orderly. Twice each week the patient is taken by wheelchair into an exceptionally clean and well-equipped shower room. A well -trained CNA assures that the shower is completed without injury. Apart from rare cases where the patient is quarantined, patients are encouraged to invite visitors. A dining room is available for ambulatory patients.

For residents living independently a dining room serving three meals a day, seven days a week is an essential. Waited service must be provided. A cafeteria line or buffet will not meet the needs of residents. Quality of food served is a vital factor in determining the success of the community.

Menu variety, the quality of food purchased and the skill of those doing the preparation all contribute to the success of the dining service. Enlightened management of the CCRC recognize the importance of allocating enough funds to this important function to, achieve maximum satisfaction from their residents.

My understanding of what the responsibilities of an executive director of a CCRC include the recruitment of individuals who will provide the management of the service to residents in all three areas-independent living, assisted living and skilled nursing.

The director is responsible for the maintenance of the infrastructure of the facility. Employees with the ability to accomplish this should be on staff.

Safety is a concern of most residents. The director must develop procedures and provide the personnel to accomplish this need.

Dining service affects every resident, three times a day, seven days a week. No CCRC will be successful unless it has a well-managed, high quality dining service. The amount of the fee paid by residents that is designated for dining service will affect its quality.

A well-managed CCRC will provide a variety of activities

both on and off campus. The morale of residents reflects the success of activities provided for them.

The director should maintain a process for monitoring the health of each resident. The director should not be limited to reports from family members on the residents' health.

Most CCRCs have a well-equipped gym. A trained individual should be in attendance to explain how the equipment is used and prevent injury.

Here at CBTS the second level of management consists of nine directors: Health Services, Life Enrichment, Resident Relations, Care Center Nursing, Human Resources, Marketing, Dining Services, Environmental Services, Fitness & Wellness.

Under the direction of the executive director, the performance of each of these seven directors contribute to the overall success of the community. A CCRC is too complicated an enterprise for any one individual to be able to manage successfully.

Unless you should have a health problem, the three directors you would be m most likely to encounter are activities, fitness, and dining services.

A CCRC In Long Beach

We knew from the last census that Long Beach was ripe for the development of a well operated retirement community. We decided to apply the profit we had earned from the sale of Warm Sands to establish a retirement community in Long Beach.

Our attorney informed us that if we would set up a charitable remainder trust we would be able to defer the payment of capital gains tax on the profit from Warm Sands. We would have to have a trustee to administer the trust. He gave us two choices; find a trustee or become the trustee ourselves. We tried many options among which was the Kendal corporation, which was operating two, what came to be known as Continuing Care Retirement Communities, henceforth referred to as a CCRC, in Eastern Pennsylvania. Their V. P. for development agreed to work with us. We met with their top people and got strong interest in becoming the owner/operator of a CCRC in the Long Beach area. When they met with their board of directors, the idea was turned down. The board did not want to commit their resources that far from home.

We tried several other possibilities in our effort to get a trustee. One of them was Friend's House in Santa Rosa. We did a lot of travelling, made a lot of phone calls, and went to a lot of meetings. In the final analysis we ended up becoming the trustees ourselves. This resulted in the formation of the Richie Family Revocable Trust. Our assets are now recorded in the name of this trust. Particularly good legal work by our attorney.

Annie's parents were then living in a CCRC, her mother was 73 when they moved there. Annie's father was 78. Her mother lived to be three weeks short of one hundred. Her father was ninety-four when he died. Her mother lived independently until she died. The last two years of her father's life were spent in the skilled nursing department. It became apparent to us that in addition to good genes, it was the lifestyle and the combined services that the CCRC provided that contributed to their longevity.

Our desire to establish a CCRC in Long Beach had not dimmed. We could not let the discouragement of Kendal's decision not to get involved prevent us from continuing our effort.

During the time we worked with Kendal we learned that we needed to recruit an advisory group to help get support from the community. I asked people from the City government, the newspaper, and the school district to work with us in an advisory capacity.

The first step was to find a plot of land that would be suitable for this purpose. It should be large enough to provide parking for the ubiquitous California drivers. It should be accessible to well-travelled streets. Price had to be a factor. The advisory group agreed with these specifications. They also agreed that any undeveloped land that met these specifications would be out of our reach. The University where I had worked had a portion of its campus that met the specifications.

It was proposed that the campuses of the University and the Veterans' Hospital be investigated as possible location for the project. Meetings with people at the University produced a lot of interest. They could see the opportunity for faculty to conduct research among the residents of the retirement community. Students could serve internships. The residents would have easy access to concerts and athletic events. The campus would provide a safe place to walk.

When we met with the administrators whose approval would be needed, we learned that a group of very liberal faculty members would protest the development of the parcel of the campus we had identified as meeting our specifications. They believed the parcel to be on Native

American burial grounds. They would protest any effort to develop the parcel. All other undeveloped parts of the campus were fully committed. Next consideration would be the Veterans' Hospital

We learned that a portion of the undeveloped campus was being leased to the University for student parking and it was possible for us to lease enough space for our project.

Our first meeting with the medical director of the hospital was very encouraging. He could see the advantages to his organization of having access to an older population, many of whom would be veteran. He also sensed that there would be a public relations benefit, something the VA would be grateful to receive.

The director called a meeting of his department heads, giving me the opportunity to make my pitch. He concluded the meeting by instructing his people to go back to their shops and come up with a report of ways in which they could contribute to our project. Who could ask for anything more?

The meeting had been held on a Friday. The following Monday I received a call from the director's secretary informing me that the director had resigned to begin his retirement.

We met with successive directors over the next few years

but none of them gave us any meaningful support. What can I say? We gave it our best shot. As I wrote the last entry into the journal that I had kept, I said that I continued to believe that Long Beach was ripe for and would benefit from a CCRC.

Making Our Choice

The reader may wonder if I will ever get around to writing about life in a retirement community. I want you to understand why it will be a CCRC where we plan to spend our golden years. I also want the reader to understand what makes a CCRC such a desirable place to be for those years.

Foulkeways, the CCRC that Annie's parents moved into, was the first of its kind and became the model for many communities that followed. A bequest of the forty acres required that they be developed for service for the elderly. The Philadelphia Yearly Meeting of Friends (Quaker) was charged with the responsibility of determining how this service might be provided. A committee comprised of lawyers, architects and bankers was formed. See above for my description of Annie's parents experience living in Foulkeways. It is proof of the success of the committee's efforts.

We visited more than 20 CCRC's. We tried to time our visit around mealtime. We would usually be invited to be a guest in their dining room. We would learn about the quality of food and service and of equal importance, the friendliness of the community. The church oriented not for profit communities were friendlier to visitors than those that were operated for profit.

We would have preferred to be in a Quaker community, but none was available on the West coast. Our four children and all but two of our eight grandchildren live on the West coast. Our choice of CCRC would be on the West coast. Our quality of life has been enhanced by having frequent visits from our extended family.

We confined our list of possibilities to those that had been accredited by a non-profit organization located in Washington, DC. I had faith in this organization when I saw the name of the executive director of Foulkeways on the list of people doing the accrediting.

There are three CCRC's in Santa Barbara. One is operated by a foundation of retired teachers. I was disappointed in the food at this community. I remind the reader that working with food, its preparation and service, had been the essence of my career.

The one operated by the Baptists was ruled out because they wanted every resident to be a member of the Baptist Church.

The third community was very up-scale and the residents were very wealthy. We would not be comfortable living there.

Long Beach has no CCRC as noted earlier.

The Presbyterians operate a community adjacent to the University of California Irvine. A retired faculty member from Cal State Long Beach, whom I knew, was a resident. We had lunch with her and were favorably impressed. This community was a possibility.

In the days when Carlsbad by the Sea was a resort town, a large three-story building that was one block removed from the Pacific Ocean was operated as a retirement community by the Lutheran Church. We were invited for lunch. I was the only man in the dining room. The building was in repair. We learned that the Lutheran Foundation was making plans to raze this building and replace it with a state-of-the-art facility.

Annie's eyes lit up with this bit of information. She really wanted to live on the water.

There was one old building right on the sand in San Diego. It had been a hotel. The rooms had been converted to efficiency apartments with pullman kitchens. The residents were required to pay for three meals a day. This requirement ruled it out. We still able to enjoy a variety of dining experience.

We were still in the information gathering phase. It would be several years before we were ready to move in to a CCRC. We had great hopes for the Carlsbad location and kept an eye on how that project developed.

Fast forward to the year 2000. A brand-new building stood on the grounds where that old hotel had stood, in Carlsbad, just one block from the ocean. We were invited for lunch. The food was great. Several of the residents spoke to us and told us how much they enjoyed living there.

Annie will never decide on something as important as this one without researching it carefully and patiently. We made several visits to Carlsbad. We spent the night at a Motel 6. We wanted to learn as much as we could about the city and what it offered. We were pleased by the charm of the village, as it was known. A variety of restaurants, retail shops and bookstores resulted in a shopping experience that was much more pleasant than having those experiences in a mall. The post office was within walking distance.

The Amtrak railroad track ran right through Carlsbad, less than half of a mile from the door of the retirement community. We learned that in addition to Amtrak trains there was commuter service throughout the day to San Diego.

Annie was now happy that with all she had learned. This was the place for us.

It was time for me to do my due diligence.

I had the need to do some research about the management of the CCRC. We had learned that an entry fee of several hundred thousand dollars was required. It was non-refundable. This was in addition to monthly dues of two or three thousand dollars made it noticeably clear that we needed significant assets to assure us that we could meet our obligations should we become residents.

During the years that we were operating the motel in Palm Springs, I became involved in the home-owners' association for the four condominiums we owned, across the street from the motel. I was elected president of the HOA. There are mandates passed by the State of California requiring them to fund reserves enough to replace or repair the common areas of the project. The list would include roofs, streets and sidewalks, swimming pools and any common area structures. I wanted to be sure that the reserves for the replacement and maintenance of the physical assets would be fully funded be the management of this CCRC where we would be making an exceptionally large entry fee.

While we were on the waiting list of *lookie loo's* we were invited to a picnic in the park that was near the community.

Each couple was assigned an escort who was a resident. I began asking some of my questions about finances. Our escort, a lovely lady named Nancy Smith, told me that the person for me to talk to was Mary Beth Tompane, and she introduced me to her. Mary Beth knew all about the finances.

I doubt if Mary Beth or I ate a bite at that picnic. She realized that I knew what I was talking about from my first question. She was obviously a very competent person. She had been the administrator of a large hospital in Arizona and was currently the president of the resident association. We became fast friends. I learned a lot from this lady.

Mary Beth told me that the California Lutheran Homes foundation has a strong balance sheet and the reserves are fully funded.

I had now done my due diligence and was comfortable to join with Annie to meet with Lee Rata, the director of admissions with the understanding that we were not ready to move in. That was just as well as there were no vacant apartments. This was a hot property.

Early Years

It had been four years since we made our deposit. In May of 2004 Annie convinced me that the time had come when we should move into what was now known as Carlsbad by the Sea. We learned that there seven people ahead of us on the waiting list.

We had just completed a cruise that ended in Vancouver, B.C. We were in line to pick up our luggage when our table mates, who knew of our plans to move into CBTS, pointed out another couple they had met who were planning to do the same thing. We introduced ourselves and our friendship with Jim and Corina Bush began that day.

We learned that the Bushes were number five In the waiting list. They told us they were not ready and would be taking their name off the waiting list. When the other four couples were given the opportunity to move in, they each declined. This was good news. We moved into N-213 on June 24, 2004. After two-and one-half years we transferred to S-327 where we continued to live.

We had access to our apartment beginning the 1st of June. I made 12 trips with my Chrysler convertible loaded to the gills with kitchen tools and stuff that you put in a bathroom.

We asked Tanya, the director of sales, to arrange for us to be joined by two other couples to help us celebrate our 55th wedding anniversary on June 25th. Frank and Beverly Gift, Jane and Fritz Shaw were selected to be our hosts that evening. It got us off to a good start. They were well qualified to answer our questions.

It was a tradition at CBTS to be entertained at lunch by the executive director. Dawn Larson was planning to retire the next week. I mentioned during our lunch that we had been on 67 cruises. Annie was not pleased. She does not like to brag. At the town hall meeting the following week, we were introduced as new residents. The director talked about all the cruises we had taken. There had not been a newly arrived resident for several months. CBTS had been in operation for only seven years. The original residents were comparatively young. We were welcomed by several couples who invited us to join them for meals. Several of them wanted to compare notes about cruises. We knew we had made the right choice.

On one of visits while we were doing our due diligence, I noticed several small books displayed on a shelf behind the front desk. The author was a resident named Corinne

Sawyer. I had written my memoirs during the period when we were free of property management responsibilities. I fancied myself to be an author. I was eager to meet this lady. As soon as we did meet, I knew that I was not in the same league with Corinne. She was a professor emeritus in Elizabethan literature from Clemson University in South Carolina. She and her sister Madeline were among the first residents. Their parents had spent their last years in the old facility.

When I told Corrine that I had worked at Cal State Long Beach for 20 years and had a feel for what it is like working in an academic atmosphere, she seemed to be willing to overlook my lack of graduate degrees. A friendship began that day which has been precious to me. Corinne has been an important contributor to making my life fulfilling.

I learned that Corinne is also a Life Master bridge player. She shares this knowledge with residents who want to improve their bridge game. On Saturday mornings, time is scheduled for Corinne's class. She teaches a short lesson that is accompanied by a hand-out. For those who have signed up, she arranges tables of play, with players assigned according to their ability. These classes are not for beginners. Her sister Madeline teaches beginners at the same time in another location. Annie and I attended Corinne's class regularly.

As we became acquainted with more residents it became

apparent to me that we have three things in common. First, we have been successful, or we could not have afforded the exceptionally large entry fee. Second, we are well traveled. Our table conversation revealed that we were not the only couple who had seen much of the world. Third, we were well educated. I believe that a good education is a concomitant of success. Over time we have learned that many of our fellow-residents have advanced degrees.

These are some of the residents we met that first year who made an impression.

One very colorful gentleman by the name of Jim Bivens, was being honored by the Long Beach Lifeguards Association for having been one of the oldest members who had served the greatest number of years. A banquet in Jim's honor was scheduled to be the Queen Mary. On one of his visits to CBTS, my son Doug Jr., was interested to hear about what was planned for Jim. Both he and his son Tyler had been Long Beach lifeguards. We planned to attend the banquet.

Mary Beth Tompane invited us for lunch during our first week as residents.

Ed Ames, one of the early residents, was known for his insatiable appetite for sweets. Eds' table for dinner one evening was right next to the Candlelight Room. The monthly birthday dinner was in progress. Pieces of the birthday cake were being passed around. Ed reached over to the table and grabbed a piece of cake. The hostess saw what had happened and pulled the plate with the piece of cake back to her table. An argument ensued. People nearby thought it would come to blows.

As I continue my effort to describe life in the old folks' home, it is difficult to maintain a sense of continuity or timeliness. I ask the reader to accept my" stream of con- sciousness" which is providing me with the material to tell my story.

The Bransford's, Tom and Fran, were a couple who invited us to dinner while we were newly arrived residents. They took us to their penthouse on the fourth floor for cocktails. Tom wanted us to see the model he had made of the build- ings on their farm back in Kentucky. It was beautiful work. His years of farming paid off when he was paid a handsome price for the farm by a real estate developer.

Some-time later, Tom became a patient in the Care Center. Upon his discharge he wrote a recommendation to the ex- ecutive director that something should be done to make the patent's rooms in the Care Center more attractive. He believed this would help in their recovery. He made a gen- erous contribution to kick start his recommendation. More about this issue later.

I remember the town hall meeting when Tim Wetzel, the newly appointed executive director was introduced. If anyone reading this was present that day, I believe you will agree that he made a particularly good impression. Someone observed that he would not stay long at this level. He was headed for bigger and better things.

Men's Breakfast

Soon after we moved into CBTS in June of 2004, I was informed of an activity that I might enjoy. It was called Men's Breakfast and was held in the back-dining room at 8:00 every Monday. The host was the chaplain, Phil Deming. I began attending and enjoyed meeting the men who attended regularly.

Phil lived in south San Diego and was often late getting to the breakfast. After a couple of Mondays waiting for Phil to get things started, I decided to step in and act as the host. This seems to be my traditional role as usually end of as the chairman or president of whatever group I am with. I introduced the idea of asking every new attender to tell us his story. These guys had led interesting lives. I laid the responsibility of keeping this thing going by asking each of them to be prepared, on a given week, to lead the discussion on a topic of their choice. This worked very well.

We tended to avoid political discussions. By the time we had reached the age to be living in a retirement community our political point of view was well established.

There were some who had no problem speaking up on an issue and defending their position with vigor. There were others who sat quietly enjoying the discussion but choosing not to get involved. We never knew how these guys were positioned-left or right.

Two active participants at the time I began attending Men's Breakfast were Dan Engstrom and Vic Clay.

Dan was an attorney who had spent most of his working career with a large bank Illinois. He was also a fine artist. I tried to buy one of his paintings, but they were not for sale.

Vic was a "Born again" Christian and made frequent references to his faith. He began every meal with a blessing that was shared with everyone at the table. His political views were as you would suspect.

Dan read voraciously. He was the best-informed person with respect to current events that I have ever known.

Vic flew transport planes, supplying the troop who were fighting the Japanese in New Guinea. He was a petroleum engineer and worked in Indonesia and Saudi Arabia in the oil industry after the war ended.

I have tried to set the stage for some rousing discussions

between these two men over the next several years.

Vic is 103 years old as I write these words. I eat breakfast with him frequently and enjoy his company. He has mellowed nicely and does not take himself so seriously.

I continued in this role for the next ten years, when I decided I needed to scale down and asked Bob Hartsfield to take over as host.

The Liars Club

Our dining room has tables for two, four and eight. At dinner one evening the host seated Annie and me at a table for eight. We did not know the other three couples. We enjoyed the meal and found that we were all compatible. We agreed that we would like to eat together again on the following Tuesday.

These are the names of the other six residents at the table that night: June and Justin Bowman, Sally Slocum and Walt Peale, Janet, and Al Christman.

We discovered Janet and Al had just gotten married. We kidded them about being newly-weds.

"Oh No!", said Janet. "We had been living together for fifteen years, but I would not move into this place unless we were married."

Sally and Walt had been living together for over twenty years. For tax reasons they chose not to get married.

It was decided that with our 55 years of marriage, we were the experts and would provide the marriage counseling when needed.

I was eager to learn how everyone had made their living. I knew they had to have been successful to be able to pay the large entry fee that is required to become a resident.

I started the ball rolling by telling a little bit about my food service experience.

Annie talked a bit about her 20 years as a school-nurse.

All the others agreed to tell their stories.

Janet had been in pursuit of a PhD when Al decided to retire and move into CBTS. She appeared to be somewhat disdainful of the rest of us.

Sally was a CPA. She worked for the Department of Agriculture conducting audits.

Walt worked for a commercial baking company. He was the supervisor for delivery. As a result of his job, he was familiar with my profession as we were one of his customers.

June grew up in a family of commercial fishermen in San Francisco. When it came to fish, she knew her stuff.

Justin was another CPA and managed a small accounting business. He was the least talkative of the group.

June raised the question. "How can you tell if we are telling the truth?"

Al thought that telling the truth, or not, could become a game. We should call ourselves The Liars Club.

His suggestion was agreed to. We continued to meet on Tuesday each week at dinner for several years. We had assigned seats. We never ran out of things to talk about.

I sat with my back to the wall. Janet was on my left, Sally on my right. Justin was next to Sally with Annie on his right. Al sat on Annie's right, followed by Walt who closed the circle.

Al began his contribution by telling us that he had been a combat infantry man in the army. He participated in Germany's last gasp effort toward the end of the war in a battle known as the Battle of the Bulge. He told what it been like on that Christmas Day. Their meal was K-Rations. No turkey. He had never been so cold. They did not have cold weather gear. The German tanks were running over the American lines. It was not until Patton arrived with his tanks that the tide was turned. Al said he is incredibly lucky to be alive. It was gripping story.

Al took advantage of the GI Bill and graduated from the University of Missouri with a degree in Journalism. He was commissioned by the Navy to write the biography of an admiral who had been a member of the team that developed the atom bomb. The admiral had been on board the Enola Gay, the plane that dropped the first bomb on Hiroshima. His job was to arm the bomb while they were in flight.

Al wrote the story of his family. His father was a barnstormer. These were fearless pilots who put on air shows, performing life threatening maneuvers as a means of entertainment. They would charge $1 to anyone who wanted a short ride in one of their primitive planes.

Al found a receptive audience in me. He shared some more of his life experiences. He ran away from home as a young teen-ager during the height of the Depression. Hitching rides in railroad box cars and staying away from the railroad cops were adventures that I could hardly imagine.

His father was abusive-of his wife and of his children. He wrote about his family and his efforts to protect them from their father.

Throughout our time here at CBTS, Al Christman was the most colorful and interesting resident of all that I can remember.

Al's death in 2007 put an end to the Liars Club. He provided the energy that had kept it going.

The Philanthropy Committee

Soon after we moved in, I was asked to become a member of the Philanthropy Committee. I was told that the primary function of the committee is to act in an advisory capacity to the directors of the California Lutheran Homes Foundation. The Foundation served as the legal entity that was able to borrow the funds needed to establish CBTS. I believe that the committee was just window dressing. The board of directors of the Foundation will do as they please.

An unspoken, but implied purpose of the committee, was for its members to contribute to the Foundation.

The day I attended my first meeting, these are the folks who were present: Don Harvey and Frank Gift, co-chairs, Corinne Sawyer, Lee Hekkala, Eric Cozens, Valerie Cumming, Ray Killeen, and Joan Johnson.

There was an agenda that had been prepared by Don and Frank.

The usual request for additions or corrections to the minutes of the previous meeting was greeted with a motion to approve the minutes. They had been prepared by Valerie who had volunteered to be the recording secretary for the committee. Valerie is competent at everything she undertakes.

Ray Killeen moved that the committee begin a project to respond to the recommendation, including a bequest, from Tom Bransford that the condition of the patient rooms in the Care Center be improved. Being a medical doctor, Ray is acutely aware of the effect that the condition of the patient's room can affect his/her recovery.

Ray made this his personal project and worked diligently for the next several years to get the funds that were needed to make the improvements. A consultant was hired who specialized in the design of hospital rooms.

Having been a patient both before and after the improvements were made, I can report as to the success of Rays efforts.

Every room had a state-of the art hospital bed. New cabinetry had been installed providing space for the patient's possessions. The walls had been painted in a variety of colorful pastel shades. No changes were needed for the bathrooms.

Ray can be immensely proud of the changes that have been made to our Care Center.

The Scholarship Program

Despite it having been ten years from the time I retired from my job at Cal State Long Beach until we moved into CBTS, I was still a devout believer in the significance that education plays in developing and maintaining a successful society. Early in our days at CBTS, I inquired as to whether there was a scholarship program for employees. I was told that yes, there had been a scholarship program but that it had died for lack of leadership. Ah hah! Here was my chance to become involved.

My first step was to get some money. I met with the Residents Association and made them aware of what I wanted to do. Would they get the scholarship program started with the modest sum of $10,000? There was unanimous approval for my efforts; however, they explained that their budget for the year had already been allocated. They suggested that I make an appeal for funds directly to our residents.

The response to my letter was gratifying. Our residents have a big heart, as well as for many of us, deep pockets.

Three residents responded to my request for committee members to join in the newly established scholarship program for our employees. Betty Roberts, Jewel Tuberville, and John Sanders signed up.

Our first task was to develop an application form that would get the applicants moving in the right direction.

We agreed that an applicant should have been on the payroll for at least six months to be eligible. They should also work a minimum of eight hours in each of those months. This would eliminate the casual employee. Our goal is to strengthen the quality of our work force by encouraging employees to stay on the job. We gave room on the application to tell us how they plan to use the scholarship money and what their goal is. For example, a Certified Nursing Assistant (CNA), might aspire to become a Licensed Vocational Nurse (LVN). The application required them to record the name of the institution that would provide the instruction. The institution must be accredited. There are too many "fly by night" money making outfits looking to steal peoples' money.

We recognized that the Director of Human Relations is the person who is in the best position to make newly hired employees aware of our scholarship program.

We got off to a slow start but when word of the program

became known we began receiving a steady stream of applications.

I continued as chair of the committee for ten years. During those years we granted over $150,000 in scholarships. We never had difficulty getting contributions to the program. Mike and Lynn Homes, who had worked in education all their professional lives, agreed to take on the leadership of the committee.

Toward the end of my time as chair, I recognized an opportunity to raise some money that would not come from residents. When Gary Wheeler retired, a man named John Workman was appointed as his successor. John was invited to our Men's Breakfast. I "buttonholed" John after the breakfast. I told him about our scholarship program and how it was increasing the productivity of the Front Porch employees who took advantage of the program. I said it would be appropriate for Front Porch to contribute to the program. He promised to get back to me. This is the procedure he suggested that would give us some contributions. The Lutheran Homes Foundation would match, up to $10,000 of the contributions from residents each year. We accepted willingly. As far as I know this process has been in effect ever since.

Hitting our Stride

We developed a routine that we followed for several years. By 7:00 AM we were out the door to begin our walk. When we started down the ramp to the beach we frequently ran into Anne Sypien and Alice Sprung who had finished their walk. It was exactly one mile to Tamarack.

We encountered many of the same people on these walks and struck interesting conversations. One gentleman was a Russian émigré. He was a teen-ager living in Leningrad during the siege of that city by the German army. He was one of a few fortunate teen-agers who were smuggled out of the city at night. If he had stayed be might have starved to death. After the war ended, he graduated from an art institute and became a successful architect after he arrived here in this country.

At that time of our lives, we were in our mid-seventies, we could walk unaided. We came home by way of Starbucks and each got our favorite drink. There was a group of regulars there who sat around on the sidewalk swapping stories.

Gail was one of the regulars. Her husband had a biking partner who was getting ready to retire. Gail had heard me talk about how happy we were living at CBTS. I suggested to Gail that we would enjoy entertaining the two couples for dinner. More to follow about what happened after that dinner.

When CBTS first opened in 1998 there was an area on the main floor off the lobby that was called the Resource Center. It had shelves for books, but no books. It was up to us, the residents to provide the books. That first year the shelves were filled with books donated by residents. When a library committee was established it received a budget each year that enabled its members to keep the library stocked with purchases.

The hospitality committee provides a welcoming service to new residents. Its chair will greet new residents and provide a well-informed litany of what to expect and how the game is played as residents. As the years passed it became a custom for the hospitality committee to host a party for a well-respected staff member who is retiring.

The activity committee works with the Director of Activities in responding to residents' suggestions and requests. Trips to ball games, museums, wineries, restaurants, the symphony, live theater, & movies are typical activities that are planned. Management allocates a portion of our monthly rent to activities, but the funding that comes from Le Cage, (more about this to follow) by way of the Residents Association, enables this committee to be more effective. The funding is used to pay for the CBTS that provides the transportation.

One of the most popular activities has been a casino that is set up in our large meeting room by a professional company. They bring in the equipment needed to operate roulette, craps, blackjack etc. Each player is given play money. Prizes are awarded to those with the most winnings at the end of the evening. Great fun!

The time came when we needed walkers to give us the stability that prevented a fall. The next step for Annie was to get a large heavy-duty electric scooter. We have a wonderful picture of her as she drives her scooter down the ramp to the beach with a look of pure delight on her face.

We did not intend to become lazy people. It was our plan to become involved in activities, both on and off campus. Annie encouraged me develop a routine of exercising in the well-equipped gym. I started out with a machine called Nu Step that required you to use both arms and legs as she moved back and forth on a bicycle seat. Resistance to your effort could be adjusted according to your desire for exercise. I worked my way up slowly so that I was on the machine for thirty minutes three times a week. There were several more machines each designated to work specific muscles in your arms and legs. The work I had done while we operated the motel had put me in good shape. I lost that during ten years after we sold the motel. My goal was to get back into that same good shape.

Monthly Walks

Two of our residents, Don, and Joyce Harvey, sponsored a monthly walk to an area well known to them. Our bus was used to get us to the trail head. The kitchen provided picnic lunches on the days when the site of the walk included a picnic bench area. They selected walks that were in city, county, or state parks, and as a result well maintained. They had clean restrooms, which for many of us was a necessity. Don would lead the more aggressive walkers while Joyce made sure that the rest of us did not get lost. She usually ended up baby-sitting the Richie's as we were the slowest walkers. She was very good about it, never complained.

Living where we do, we appreciate being close to the Pacific Ocean. We also enjoy the quaintness of the Carlsbad Village. Now with these walks we are learning to appreciate the beauty of some the un-developed area of North San Diego county. We joined up at the appointed hour to eat our lunch. We had fun comparing notes about what we had seen. Some of us proved to be much more observant. I participated in these walks as long-as we were able to walk unaided. In this way we got to see a lot of the beautiful countryside in north San Diego County.

The Harveys deserve a lot of credit for this contribution to our community.

The Del Mar Racetrack

Another activity was Annie's favorite. Once each summer during the horse racing season, a trip to the racetrack in the San Diego Fairgrounds was scheduled. She would spend the morning of that day handicapping the races. She made careful notes for the seven races that we stayed for. Everyone was tired by that time and we left early. We took the elevator to the fourth level where we could get a space for handicapped people without having to climb up and down stairs to get to the betting windows.

We moved up to the handicap section. Annie would prepare the bet, usually two or three dollars for a horse to place or show. It was my job to run her bet over to one of the windows. She was so pleased with herself when her bet made a little money. She enjoyed herself for the next six races and always came home having made a little profit. It was a cheap way to have a lot of fun.

The Chime Choir

An activity that I enjoyed was the chime choir. Someone had donated a set of chimes to the community. Chimes are less expensive than bells, but they are used for the same purpose. There were 16 chimes in the set. It required a minimum of eight players with each plyer handling two chimes. Not all the members in our choir could play two chimes. As I remember we had about twelve players. Shirley Cameron was the musically talented resident who organized and recruited the residents to participate. The ability to read music and the willingness to commit time and energy to the rehearsals, were stipulated by Shirley, to become a member of the choir. She was a tough task master. For the first several weeks she tried to be the director while playing two chimes. Jim Sharp was a resident who had majored in music in college. Jim was drafted to be the conductor. He did very well and enjoyed the activity. The day came when Shirley decided we were ready to give a concert. The audience of residents were very forgiving our occasional mistakes and gave us a standing ovation for our efforts.

Bingo

When I talked about Jim Sharp being the conductor of the chime choir, I am reminded that Jim was also known as "Mr. Bingo." Once a month on Friday night a sign would appear at the Front Desk announcing Bingo Tonight.

Fifteen to twenty of us regulars would hurry down to the multi-purpose room where Jim was waiting for us to sell us our Bingo cards. $1.00/card. I bought six cards. Ray and Mary Killeen were usually sitting on the left end of the front row. Annie and I sat next to them. Walt Peale sat on the right end of the first row.

Corinne was always there, in her same seat. I could never understand why Corinne played this game as highly intelligent as she is. Maybe it is for the sociability. She always seems to be having a good time and nearly always wins at least one game. There were Bingo nights when I really did not want to play what I felt was a silly game. Annie loved it. I had to suck it up and keep her happy. As they say, 'Happy wife, happy life.'

Bowling

Next came an activity that we both enjoyed. It was called Wii Bowling. It uses technology to create the sensation of going to an actual bowling alley. A small electronic device is held and enables the player to swing his arm back as though he were going to throw a real bowling ball. The difference is the device weighs but a few ounces. The sights and sounds are so authentic you think you are really bowling.

Frank Gift is responsible for getting our Wii bowling program set up and running. Frank is a Cal Tech graduate and very smart. He had been bowling in a public bowling alley and knew what fun it is as well as being good exercise. When he heard about the Wii bowling program, he could see that it would work very well here at CBTS.

Frank enlisted the help of Bill Knowles. Together they developed a system of handicapping that enabled every participant to be competitive.

Frank gave a talk about the program at one of our bi-weekly town hall meetings. He needed six volunteers to serve as team leaders. Remember, this was all happening when CBTS had just coming alive. We were comparatively young.

Frank got his six volunteers. The next step was to get participants. He reasoned that it would take six teams of at least six members on a team to make the program run effectively.

One of our residents had retired from a successful career as a general contractor. Al Zeis is one of these people who does everything well. He was one of the first people who tried his hand at Wii bowling. He bowled a perfect score, a 300.

He saw that Annie was trying to figure out how to use the controller. Being the kind of guy, he is, Al offered to help. She caught on quickly. By the second week of this exciting new activity, Annie was getting scores in the low 200's. She was beating all the men. She had a strange delivery. She took two or three practice strokes before releasing the ball and then fairly leaping toward the screen. Annie was bowler of the year for the next two years. I was proud of her.

We have two large screen TV' side-side-by-side in our multi-purpose room. This enables two teams of four players each to be competing at the same time. A second pair of teams will be ready to compete when the first match is over. There will be lots of cheers and cat calls from the audience throughout the competition. Everyone is having a good time, especially those on the winning teams.

The two large screen TVs would enable you to watch the progress of your competitor.

At its height of popularity, there were six teams of six plyers each. Four teams compete each evening, one pair at 5:30, the second at 6:30.

Several married couples signed up. They would not be assigned to the same team, it made for good fun when they competed. Among these were Carol and Blair Benjamin, Virgil and Barbara Carlson, Wally and Dottie Cohan, Don and Joyce Harvey, Ray and Mary Killeen, Chuck and Hilde Rankin, Norman and Alice Sprung, Gene and Wilma Wetzel and Annie and Doug Richie.

There many single bowlers whose names bring back some memories. Willy Leventhal was one of those. I can still hear him shouting out, "Be there! Be there!" referring to a strike.

John Uhlig was another. I first met John when I was parking in the downstairs garage. I parked next to a vintage four door Cadillac. A fine-looking gentleman, dressed in coat and tie, was getting out of the car. He introduced himself. He told he had just returned from getting his driver's license renewed. He went on to tell me that he had been turned down when he went to the local DMV office. He was unable to turn his head to see out of the rear window when he did as instructed and started to back up. You cannot depend on the rear-view mirrors, he was told. He did not pass that day.

John had been told that the DMV office in Temecula was much more forgiving of older people. He had driven to Temecula and got his renewal. John was 94 at the time of this story. He had been the pastor of a Lutheran church for 40 years. His congregation loved him and came to visit him frequently.

John was dependent on using a wheelchair by this time. You would not believe it if you had not seen it, but he could bowl from his chair. He must have been an athlete. He bowled in the high 100's consistently.

Another resident who bowled with difficulty was Wilma Wetzel, the mother of our first executive director, Tim Wetzel. Wilma was frail. You wondered if she was going to be able long enough to finish her game. She was courageous and never let her team down.

Carol Benjamin was a tiny woman. As my mother used to say, she would not weigh 100 pounds soaking wet. To add insult to injury, she carried an oxygen pack on her back. We watched her struggle to get up to the line when it was her turn to bowl. Blair, her husband, made no effort to help her. As we watched this couple, we could see that this was the way that she wanted. One night as she took her first turn, she fell. Everyone gasped. Surely Blair would come to her rescue. He did not. She struggled back to her feet and finished her session. What a lesson of courage it was for all of us that night.

So that more of you will get your jollies when you read this book, I will mention as many of you who are still with us, that I remember as being bowlers.

Jackie Allen, Taylor Balance, Yvonne Dirks, Frank Gift, Ralph Pegors, Corinne Sawyer, Jane Shaw, Anne Sypien, Mary Thompson, and Maggie Wolever.

There is one more resident who was the champion bowler without question. Her name is Evelyn Williams. She had been a trust officer in a major bank in New York City. Despite being African American with a distinct southern accent, she succeeded in a profession dominated by men.

I was there the first day that Evelyn came to bowl. It took her awhile to get the hang of the controller. By the end of her first game she was getting some strikes. I tried to encourage her and urged her to come back next week.

I do not know if she practiced during the next few days,

but the next Tuesday Evelyn was throwing strikes all over the place. She bowled her first perfect game that week. She seemed to be able to bowl a perfect game whenever she chose. Evelyn showed up every night that bowling was scheduled, even if her team was not scheduled to bowl. She would gladly offer help someone who asked. She never criticized. She was a wonderful addition to our community.

Life Histories

Don and Joyce Harvey received a grant from the California Lutheran Homes Foundation that provided the equipment needed to photograph the subject while being interviewed. The result was a DVD. Copies were made for family members. Don did the photography and spent hundreds of hours edited the result. Joyce prepared an outline for the interview and prompted when necessary. Copies of the finished product were made for each family members. We each participated and are glad we did. We owe a sincere vote of thanks to Don and Joyce.

I was surprised to learn that Annie had talked much longer than I did. She has been kidding me for years that I dominate the conversation when we are with a group. She never gets to say a word. This was her chance. Don presented us with fully edited DVD's of our conversations with enough copies for each of our children.

This project took a substantial amount of Don and Joyce's time and energy. We have much to be thankful for a result.

Portrait Painters

Several of our residents were fine artists. Apart from Dan Engstrom, they were all women. On most mornings, after the dishes are done, several of them would gather in the arts and crafts room on the first floor of the main building.

Our community is a virtual rumor mill. The word was out that several of the artists were looking for models so they could paint portraits. My Annie always has her ear to the ground. She said I would be a great model. They would love to have me.

There is one artist who painted two different views of the exterior of the main building. They are displayed in the executive suite. She is the only one of our artists who made a living from the sale of her work. She is a graduate of Smith College. I have a soft spot in my heart for Smith graduates. I have yet to meet one who was not special. Annie's good friend Sue Silva is an example.

There were four artists painting that morning. I was hoping that the Smith graduate's work would be such that I would want to buy it, but I was disappointed. She is not a portrait artist. The one that I really liked was pencil work by Janet Christman. She had been one of the regular attenders at the Liar's' Club dinners.

Badminton in the Pool

There was one resident who made an immediate impression on me. I was barely in the lobby on my first day when big bear of a man accosted me. His name was Willie Levanthal. Our friends from the yacht club in Long Beach had warned me to be on the look-out for a man named Willy. From the way they had escribed him I knew this was the guy. His first words were "The beard's got to go, and you need a haircut. I think I had a good response."When you can wear my belt, I will do both of things." I am still bearded and longhaired as I write these words.

Willy invited me to join the game of water badminton that occurred in the pool behind the Grand Building every Saturday morning.

I accepted his invitation and participated in that activity for several years. My first partner was Mary Thompson. She had been a varsity tennis player as an undergraduate at Stanford.

I looked forward to those Saturday morning games and continued to play while I was physically able.

Willy's usual partner was an older gentleman named Carlin Matson. He had practiced dentistry for over 45 years. Several of our residents had been his patients. Carlin was a graduate of USC, both undergraduate and the school of dentistry.

The day was coming when Carlin would celebrate his 100th birthday. He and his wife Ruthie were an extremely popular couple. Their daughter Wendy, as is our Wendy, is a nurse. She and Ruthie wanted to make Carlin's birthday special. They turned to one of our residents who is also an SC graduate.

The celebration was planned for a Friday when we were having one of our happy hours. It was about 5:30 that afternoon when everyone had had a couple of drinks. Beginning from the South corridor behind the front desk, the sound of a brass band could be heard. As the group providing the music moved toward the lobby the volume increased. There were three trumpets and five trombone and drums. Anyone who has been at an SC football game or watched those games on TV is familiar with the tune. It is called Conquest. It is SC's fight song. They blew the roof off our lobby. Anyone who was there that day will never forget it. Nor will we forget those obnoxious SC fans who call themselves Trojans.

I was interrupted at this point by my care giver telling me

that my dinner was on the table. Have I failed to tell you that our children have arranged for me to have round the clock care givers?

As I enjoyed my dinner, I looked across the room to see the beautiful poinsettia plant that our friend John Ciullo gave us. He delivered it the week before Christmas. Thanks to the care received from my care givers, it is flourishing. Perhaps it is the location in the room where it gets afternoon light. Maybe it has something to do with sunlight and chlorophyll.

A bit more about my new friend Willy. He spent part of everyday in our care center where his wife was a patient. Elise has MS. Willy had moved some of her furniture into her room. He repainted it and made it as attractive as possible. This is a man with a big heart.

Willy and Elise had been living in what is described as a 55+senior living community called Ocean Hills Country Club. The homes were individually owned. There was a golf course, tennis court and pickleball courts. Two club bouses were available for pre-arranged social events. The public areas were maintained by the association to which the residents paid dues. There was no medical care.

Ocean Hills became a springboard for people to move to CBTS. I cannot put a number to the number of couples who made that move, but there have been many.

Bus Tours

Dialing the clock back a bit I want to tell about an activity that occurred early in those first years.

I received a long hand-written invitation from a resident named Pete Peterson. It was an invitation for us to join on one of his chartered bus tours. He went into detail about the qualifications of the bus and the tour leader who was provided by the bus company. His group, although less than half the number needed to fill the bus, would receive preferential treatment.

His next trip would go to Bryce Canyon, returning through Zion Canyon. We had visited these places on our tour of the national parks in 1944. Still, the idea of a guided tour excited our interest. We signed up and were glad that we did.

My stability had begun to waiver. I was walking with a cane. Pete assured me that I would be the first on and first off, the bus. My reserved seat would be in the front row next to the window on the door side. The tour leader would have the seat behind the driver. I was baffled by all this special treatment I was receiving.

Everything that Pete had promised came to be. I guess Annie was nervous. She had to use the restroom on the bus before we got going. She gave it a good report.

Pete's wife Joyce acted as our Hostess. She passed doughnuts and coffee around, enough for everybody, including those not in his group. She had been a pre-school teacher. She welcomed us each morning with a ditty that she sang. "Good Morning to you!"

As the hours passed, we began to appreciate the reason for Pete having been so specific about the specifications of the bus. The air conditioning worked, and it was a wonderfully comfortable ride.

It became apparent that first morning that our tour guide not only knew her stuff, but she had a great sense of humor.

Those of you who have never taken a bus tour, I assure you that the days can be long. A competent tour leader makes all the difference between having a good experience and being bored to death.

Before we moved to CBTS we had taken a bus tour that started in Portugal, crossed through Spain, and then crossed the Mediterranean into Morocco. The bus driver was

Spanish and spoke little English. There was no tour speaker. Had it not been for one of our members who spoke beautiful Spanish, this tour would have been much less enjoyable

Getting back to the Petersen tour, it took two full days of driving to reach our hotel outside of Bryce. A planned bus stop was at a restaurant that had a small casino. We were in Utah. Gambling is legal here Many small businesses installed a few slots. A few people from out bus took advantage of the opportunity to lose some money. I was not one of them.

We arrived at Bryce in late afternoon, just in time to enjoy the spectacular sunset on those red sandstone spires,

Our driver qualified to enable us to be driven down into the canyon. These are sights to be seen that were not visible from the rim of the canyon. We began the next day on the floor of Zion Canyon. The National Park Service provides tour leaders for groups of more than 20 visitors. Our tour leader was a geologist. She not only knew her subject; she had a great sense of humor. There was a second tour in the afternoon for those who desired. I chose to take a nap. I had heard enough geology to last a while.

The route back to Carlsbad took us through Las Vegas. It was common knowledge that you could get a particularly good meal at reasonable prices at any casino in the city. Our tour leader set a time for returning to the bus. She did not want to keep a busload waiting while one of her riders got involved in playing the slots.

It was a tired, but happy, busload that pulled into CBTS about five that afternoon.

Annie and I would live to take one more bus tour with Pete and Joyce.

Senor Staff

As you leave our apartment, taking the elevator to the second floor, and walk toward the lobby, you will pass a group of eight photographs. These are the eight people who comprise the senior staff These are the people who are responsible for providing the service that is promised when you become a resident of a CCRC.

Joan Johnson is the Executive Director. She is the boss. She supervises the other seven people whose pictures are displayed.

Joan has settled into her job with a sense of confidence. She instituted a weekly session that is called "Rumor has it". Any resident is encouraged to attend. Joan answers all the questions honestly and frankly.

The directors of Health Services and Resident Relations are two people with whom I have had no contact. I will make no comment about what they do and how well they may be doing it.

Sue Macango is the Head Nurse. In this capacity she is the manager of the Care Center, as our skilled nursing facility is known. Sue runs a tight ship. She expects each of her employees to meet the high standards that she has set. She has a nice sense of humor and a big heart. She and Joan are good friends. This works to the benefit of all of us.

When the Care Center is full, it generates a surplus revenue. This can help to reduce the amount of increase in the rent that we all pay.

Sue has the job of keeping enough beds empty so that residents who become ill or undergo surgery will be taken care of.

One of the reasons for Sue's success is the weekly meeting she holds with all her team leaders. I compare this to grand rounds in a hospital. She discusses each new patient and the plan for their treatment. They are encouraged to ask questions and make comments. I believe these weekly meetings have much to do with the success of the Care Center.

The Care Center has an excellent reputation in north San Diego county. Hospitals have confidence that the patients that they discharge can be referred to our Care Center with the assurance they will receive excellent care.

The therapy department is outsourced. It also has an

excellent reputation. Every patient in the Care Center receives some physical and occupational therapy. I benefit from this service. It hastened the time when I could be discharged.

Sue Feehan is the Director of Fitness and Wellness. She has an outgoing, sunny disposition that makes you happy to be in her presence. Sue is responsible for the operation of the very well-equipped fitness center. Here are machines designed to stress every muscle in your body. Instruction and guidance in the use of the equipment is essential to avoid injury. Sue is eminently qualified for this job. She is an exercise physiologist and has studied kinesiology.

Sue has been putting her creative talent to work during this time of difficulty for all of us. She has developed exercises that we can perform at home, complete with drawings to demonstrate now they work. She is encouraging us to keep active as a means of avoiding becoming discouraged during this time of being alone in our apartment.

Sue could have taken a vacation now that the gym is closed. Instead she has put her creative ability to work to help us get through the quarantine.

We are fortunate to have Sue Feehan as our Director of Fitness and Wellnesses, we look forward to the day when the quarantine is over, and the gym is back in operation.

Ozzie Nelson is the Director of Activities. She is also one of those special people who is always happy. Her enthusiasm infectious.

Ozzie solicits suggestions for activities. She uses sigh-up sheets to determine if there is sufficient interest to plan the event. Her job then becomes arranging for transportation and purchasing enough tickets for the event, so we will not get shutout when we arrive.

Ozzie has an extensive wardrobe which she uses to match up with whichever event she is coordinating. She participates in all the happy hours. It is her job to hire the musicians for these events. Ozzie makes a real contribution to making our life here at CBTS a joyful experience

Jamie Gerkowski is the Director of Dining Service. He and Wendy Coleman the Dining Room manager had worked together at another job. Jamie knew that the service in the dining room was under control. He would not have to be concerned with that function.

Jamie's first project was to install different form of service that he called the Bistro. It was installed along the wall beginning at the salad bar and continuing to the resource center

The Bistro combined preparation facilities with a serving

counter the principal item of equipment was a state-of-the-art oven that could bake pizza as well as hat sandwiches like Rueben's, ham, and cheese and patty melts. Milk shakes and cokes were available and an assortment of salads, could be brought in from the kitchen. Soup and chili completed he menu.

Tables for two and for were arranged against the wall opposite to the serving counter.

There was one more innovation that Janie brought to the dining service. On Wednesdays he had three six-foot tables setup in the lobby. He planned a menu for Wednesday that would include an item that could be carved, such as tenderloin of beef, leg of lamb or turkey. The chef set up station on the counter of the Bistro. Residents were already lined up to be served. The three tables would be filled before the service began.

He called this operation The Carvery.

CBTS has always enjoyed a reputation among the Front Porch communities, for our fine dining service. Now we have ever more reason to be proud and thankful.

Thank you, Jamie, for bring us an outstanding dining experience.

The Trivia Contest

One of the most popular activities since CBTS opened in 1998, has been the Trivia Contest. The format provides for four teams of residents and one team of staff. Corinne Sawyer is the quiz master.

The procedure is modelled after the TV show Jeopardy. The questions are organized by category. The difference is that the contestants work as a team, not as individuals. The team must agree on an answer. The team leader is the only one who can answer the question.

The teams are identified by a color. Two teams are selected to compete in the first session of the day. The remaining two teams will compete in the second session.

Should the team that the question was directed to be unable to answer, the opposing team gets a chance to answer.

A large score board is posted on the wall where everyone can see it.

The audience is supposed to keep quiet, even when one of them knows the answer to a question. That rule is hard to enforce.

The contest starts on the first Wednesday in August and continues for three more weeks. There is a tremendous amount of work required by the quiz master to have many questions at her fingertips. Corinne deserves a lot of credit for continuing to perform as quiz master.

Her job begins when she organizes the teams. She has a remarkable knowledge of our relative ability of the folks who have signed up. She puts the teams together with an equal distribution of talent. A captain is designated. Each team is assigned color-Red, Blue, Green and Gold. We are ready to go.

She prepares a compilation of the names and captains of all four teams that is sent to each of the contestants. The staff is left to organize their team.

The tradition has been for the team captains to schedule a meeting for their team at which they select a name and a cheer. We behave as though we were back in high school.

Bridge

Many of our residents have been bridge players before they moved in to CBTS. I suspect that most of us were unaware of the modern conventions that have made the game much more interesting.

Corinne Sawyer is a Life Master bridge player. She is also a professor emeritus from Clemson University. Thirdly, she is very generous of her time. Put this together and we have someone who can teach us and help us to learn how to use the new conventions.

On Saturday morning at 10:00 AM, several us will gather in the Resource Room. Corinne will have been there before we arrive to arrange the tables where we will be playing. She gives a short lecture explaining the topic of the day. It ends with a hand-out. Some of the topics include transfers, convenient minor bids, weak two bids, Cue bids the rule of eleven and unusual no-trump bids.

Then it is time to play bridge. She positions the players at tables where there is similar ability.

She keeps herself available for questions. Over a period of months and years, the bridge playing group of residents has enjoyed a marked improvement in our play of the game.

Every Monday afternoon people sign up for a game of what is called rubber or party bridge. You come as an individual plyer and play with whomever is seated at your table. You play eight hands and then move to another table with a new partner.

The more serious players gather on Thursday afternoons to play what is known as duplicate bridge. You need a partner to get into this game. Boards are supplied, each of which contains four pockets that each hold thirteen cards. As you play your hand, you keep the card you have just played in front of you. When the hand is finished, you put the cards have played back in the pocket. The board is then taken to anther table so another couple will be able to play the same hands. This makes it possible for there to be a context among all the couples playing that day. A director is needed to record the results from each board.

It must give Corinne some satisfaction to see players who began learning in her classes are now playing duplicate.

Couples

Early in our time at CBTS we learned of the marriage of two of our residents, Cliff, and Eloise Bagsund. They had each lost their spouse before they moved in. We had not met the couple, but the talk was they were extremely popular, and everyone was happy for them.

The rules have changed since Annie and I began our life together. Virgin brides were common. Today we have the sad situation of fourteen-year-old girls becoming mothers. Over the years we have come to see more couples choosing to live together without getting married. They see a tax advantage with this arrangement.

Two of the couples who were members of our Liars Club had been living together for many years. Janet Christman insisted on getting married to Al before they arrived at CBTS, even though they had been living together for over 20 years. Walt and Sally had been together for many years. They are known as Walt Peale and Sally Slocum. I assume they have separate contracts. Nobody cares. This is their business.

I am interrupting a bit when I tell the story of how we got Gracie.

The time came when we decided we wanted to have a cat. We wanted a short haired, mature female that had been neutered. Bill and Kit Schofield were known as the cat people. When we told them, we wanted to adopt a cat, they agreed to help us.

Bill and Kit drove us to the Oceanside animal shelter. I was amazed by the facility. It was immaculately clean. The employees were wearing uniforms. They were cheerful and appeared to be enjoying their job. We had agreed that we wanted an older short hair female that had been neutered. We were taken to the area where the cats were displayed. Each cat was in a two-compartment cage, which kept the space where the cat slept and fed separate from the litter.

There were two cats that met our specifications. As soon as I saw Gracie, I knew she was the one. All the cats have a narrative that includes their name. I am very grateful to Kit and Bill for bringing me Gracie.

When I was discharged from our skilled nursing facility after Annie died, I returned to an empty apartment no other person was living there. Gracie knew there has been a change in her life when she could not find Annie. When I moved my lounge chair into the space where Annie's chair had been, Gracie figured out that I was the one who would give her the attention she craves.

There are four spots in our apartment where Gracie hangs out. Her favorite is my lap. Here is where she gets the petting that she craves. Next comes a rocking chair that has a cushion on the seat. Third is the single bed in my office where I take my nap. Finally, she hides under the bed in our bedroom on the day the housekeeper comes to clean the apartment and brings a vacuum cleaner. Gracie does not like vacuum cleaners.

Gracie is a curious cat. She will sneak out into the corridor every chance she gets. All my neighbors have had a visit from Gracie.

She has earned a reputation. The nurses who bring me my medications all know Gracie. They expect to see her sitting on my lap being petted. They see other cats as they perform their duties throughout the complex. The know that Gracie is special.

Again, I want to thank Bill and Kit for bringing me Gracie. As long as I have her, I will not be alone.

Jack and Grace Kalberer are a remarkable couple Jack earned both an MD and Ph.D. He was basically a scientist, he never practiced medicine. He traveled all over the world on behalf of the World Health Organization, gathering knowledge about ways to treat cancer. We became good friends because we each grew up in or near New York City.

Grace taught math and science at the high school level. I know she was an excellent teacher and could tell she would tolerate no misbehaving in her classes. She has an ingratiating smile, but behind that smile is a will of iron.

There is one special couple who hit the ground running as soon as they arrived. Penny and Steve Held became involved immediately in the activities that interested them. Clear out of the blue, they presented me with a CD containing John Denver's rendition of Annie's Song. It is one of my treasured CDs.

The first time I saw Penny in action was a moment when we were serving on the Scholarship committee. Penny insisted that the institutions that were bring attended by the applicants must be accredited.

Penny had volunteered to succeed Jane Shaw as the chairman of the hospitality committee. Jane had been the chairman since CBTS opened in 1988. Penny's enthusiasm translated to the ability to explain what was in store for new residents and to encourage them to participate in the activities that interested them.

Many of you who are reading this little tale will confirm that Penny did an excellent on of welcoming new residents.

It was because I was chairman of the nominating committee that Penny came to me with this question. Could she continue as chairman of the hospitality committee if she were to be elected to the office of secretary of the resident's association board of directors? I assured her that she cold. She ran, was unopposed, and is now the secretary of the resident's association and is doing an excellent job. She gets the minutes out promptly and sees to it that they are distributed to all residents.

Penny assisted Taylor Balance and Jackie E in getting the choir organized and running. She also took over the job of posting he score on a large white board behind the quiz master for the trivia game. Gordon Sigler took a lot of flak when he did his job. He made mistakes and the audience was quick to tell him about it. Penny does not make mistakes.

Steve Held's life has been centered around music. He operated a successful music store before coming to CBTS. They sold pianos as well as other musical instruments. Steve is a percussionist. He gave the residents demonstration at one of our town hall meetings, explaining the many elements in a full set of percussion instruments. He brought other musicians along on several occasions and performed a jazz concert. He teaches young people to be become percussionists.

Steve devotes many hours each week to assisting in the moving of larger items for sale at La Cage. Gracie Spoe will attest to this. It was because of this activity that Steve was honored as the volunteer of the year for 1999. A well-deserved honor.

I want to get the name of one more man into my story. He was never a couple. This, despite the effort of a lady who shall go nameless. Soon after he moved in, Bob Walker celebrated his birthday by inviting everyone in the community to be his guest for lunch at the hotel across the street. We were unable to attend but we understand that over 100 of our residents did attend, and they had a great time. They enjoyed hamburgers with all the trimmings and there was live music.

The next year on his birthday, Bob arranged to have a Hawaiian luau set up on the courtyard at CBTS. It was followed by a performance from a group of Hawaiian dancers. Everyone was invited.

Bob did not live to celebrate another birthday, I did, however, leave funds that made it possible to have another luau and performance by Hawaiian dancers. He was one of a kind.

There are several other couples who are enjoying a relationship, each of which is quite different.

Willy Leventhal had made a name for himself while he was still living at Ocean Hills. He organized a petition to have the name of the community changed. It was then known as Ocean Hills retirement Community. With its golf course, tennis court and pickle ball courts it qualified as a country club. The change was approved and henceforth the community was known as Ocean Hills Country Club.

Willy moved into a studio apartment in our Grand Building soon after Elise was admitted to the Care Center.

Taylor Balance was a well-known resident at Ocean Hills. She was recognized for her theatrical talent as well as her lovely singing voice. As a graduate of the College of William and Mary I assume she received training while she attended the College of William and Mary that augmented her talents. She wrote a play that gave her the starring role. Willy organized a bus load from CBTS to attend the performance. It was much enjoyed.

The word was now out that Carlsbad by the Sea was the place to go when you knew you were going to need more care than you would receive at Ocean Hills.

Taylor and Willy had become good friends. She visited Willy after he moved into the Grand Building. He continued to sing the praises of CBTS. She recognized several former Ocean Hills residents now living at CBTS. They all spoke well of their decision.

Taylor moved into a penthouse unit. Her outgoing personality enabled her to be fully absorbed into our community. She did a lot of traveling and always went first class. No formal announcement was made but the careful observer could see that Willy was now living with Taylor. They were a popular couple. They seldom ate alone in our dining room.

To set the stage for introducing the next couple I will describe the location of what we called The Nook. It was on the left side wall as you approach the Resource Center. Banquettes will seat up to eight people with room at the front of the tables for three or four chairs, or walkers or in my case an electric wheelchair.

When we arrived at CBTS there were several regulars who sat in The Nook on those days when we had a happy hour.

Fritz and Jane Shaw had blue name tags signifying that they were among the first residents to come to CBTS in 1998. They were desert rats. This is what those of us who have lived in the Coachella Valley Desert call ourselves.

Frizz had been a general contractor. He worked as a real estate appraiser for Riverside County. Jane was a home economist who demonstrated appliances for Southern California Edison.

Chuck Killen had a management position in the division of the Southern California Gas Co. that delivered gas to its customers. Pat was an accomplished seamstress. She organized a group of residents who shared her ability. They made quilts for the marine families living at Camp Pendleton. Gordon Ziegler had been a Delta Airline pilot. It was reported that he was the youngest person to ever have moved into CBTS. We suspect it was to keep his money away from his two exes. Gordon was a car buff. Anyone needing information about a brand or model knew that Gordon was the guy to talk to.

Jim McNab had retired from the electrical contracting business that he created after he had moved to Alaska. Joan was his high school sweetheart while they were living in Philadelphia. When Jim's wife died, he invited Joan to come to Alaska. It must have been a proposal by 'phone. The sale of his business made him a very wealthy man. They ended up living here at CBTS for much the same reasons that brought us all here.

Joan developed pancreatic cancer and died while she was in our care center. We all loved her.

One of the more colorful residents we met soon after moving in, was Barney Hekkala. He had been gravely wounded in WWII, losing a leg. He managed to get a wooden leg to replace the missing leg. He refused offers to get a more sophisticated device. Barney died soon after we moved in.

Barney's wife Lee was the type of individual who does not function well alone. I can relate to that. I could not have imagined how I would function living without Annie.

Jim was devastated when Joan died. He was susceptible to the attention that Lee was ready to provide. It did not take long before we could see that they had become a couple. They wore matching jackets from the University of Oregon, where one of Jim's granddaughters attended. I nicknamed them the "The Bobbsey Twins."

I can never remember seeing Lee and Jim eat with anyone in our dining room. Again, quoting the rumor mill, it was passed around that they had eaten at every fine restaurant in North San Diego County. On those rare occasions when we saw them in our dining room, it was always for lunch and at a table for two.

Jim and I are of the same age. He considers me to be more than an acquaintance. We share the experience of having lived for many years in Philadelphia. He told me that he had made a nice contribution to the Scripps Encinitas Hospital. They were receiving some nice invitations to fund raisers that Scripps Health hosted. We were on that same invitation list.

We received an invitation to a dinner party at one of the Marriott Hotels. Annie was convinced that I should not drive at night. She asked Jim if we could ride with them to the party. We repeated this routine several times for more parties.

Lee is particularly good with names. Once we arrived at a party, she would be fully occupied speaking to people she knew and introducing Jim and herself to people she did not know. She never introduced us to anyone. We were left to shift for ourselves.

There was one party that resulted in a memorable experience. We were seated at a table with two couples who were residents of La Costa Glen retirement community. It is a much larger community with over 900 residents and two dining rooms. As had most of our fellow residents here at CBTS, we had visited La Costa Glen and found it to be lacking our expectations

Lester Teeny was a survivor of the Bataan Death March. He endured the torture and abuse of the Japanese soldiers while he was in a POW camp waiting to be sent to Japan to perform slave labor. He spent the next four years working twelve hours a day, seven days a week in a coal mine in Japan.

When the war ended Lester continued his education, He

earned a doctorate and joined the faculty of the school of business at Arizona State University.

Several years later Lester was singled out as one of the thousands of American soldiers who had been the victim of atrocities committed by Japanese soldiers while the Americans were being held prisoner. He was invited to attend an event hosted by the Japanese Ambassador in the Japanese Embassy in Washington, DC. An apology was extended on behalf of the Japanese government to the men and women who been the victims of the atrocities committed by Japanese soldiers during World War II. These acts were in strict defiance of the Geneva Convention.

There is no record of what was said that day, but I assume that Lester was one who rejected the apology with an emotional recitation of chapter and verse based on his personal experience.

Allan and Sue Haber moved in to one of the two beach front apartments in the ocean front building two years after we arrived. We made a point to invite new residents to join us for dinner. It was apparent that Allan was in the advanced stages of dementia. Sue confirmed our suspicion.

Allan was a judge for the Los Angeles Superior Court. He was scheduled to be the judge for the O J. Simpson trial. As the date approached for the trial to begin, it was apparent that he would not be capable of serving. Sue wept as she told us this sad story. She said Allan was brilliant. Had he been able, the results of the trial might have been quite different. She went so say that Johnnie Cochran would not have been able to twist Allan's arm in the way that he had influenced Judge Ito.

Sue is a highly intelligent woman. She had an executive position with a company that required her to fly regularly to the East coast. She was happy to be able to retire.

I have said that our residents have been successful. This applies to the three retired military officers who are with us, each of whom reached the rank of colonel. This is in indication of their high intelligence as well as their qualities of leadership. Tom Metzger retired as a Colonel from the Marine Corps.

A cute story involves our first meeting with Tom. He had begun moving into 227. His apartment has the same floor plan as ours.

There was a lot of activity around the wall that separates the living room from the master bedroom. The door to the apartment was open. Annie walked in and introduced herself to Tom. She expressed her concern that if he removed that wall, part of our apartment would come crashing down. Tom assured her that he knew the wall was a baring wall and any changes made in it would not affect its function.

There is an aphorism that says, "Cream rises to the top."

It was not long after Tom moved in that we noticed that he and Sue were eating dinner together. They continue to do so and obviously enjoy each-others company.

The next couple is a bit harder to explain. Jane Shaw had been one of our best bridge players. She teamed up with Chuck Killen. They played together for years. They were un-beatable. Chuck's ability to play well declined. He stopped playing.

Paul Saffell was a new resident who attended Corinne's Saturday morning bridge classes. He, as were we all, was learning the new conventions. Corinne assigned partners for the games that we played after the lesson. She put Paul at a table with Jane, knowing that she could continue with Paul's education.

We became used to seeing Jane and Paul together at the bridge table on Saturday morning.

One evening at dinner, Annie noticed that Jane and Paul were sitting at a table for two. This was social, not bridge.

Jane's health had begun to fall. She moved permanently into

our Care Center. Paul brought her in a wheelchair to our Saturday morning bridge games. We could see a marked improvement in Pauls' game. Janes influence was apparent.

They eat together at dinner regularly. Paul is devoted in bringing Jane down in a wheelchair. I say down, as our Care Center is on the third floor.

We are happy for them as they seem to be meeting each other's needs.

There is one more couple I want to talk about. They are no longer with us. Harry and Pola Triandises were each naturalized citizens.

Harry was born on the island of Corfu. He talked about how the occupying Italian soldiers stole all the food during World War II. The natives lived under starvation conditions. After the war ended, Harry went to Canada. He completed his high school education and was on his way to study engineering. A teacher suggested that he switch to psychology. He went to Cornell University and earned his PhD. He spent 40 years teaching psychology at the University of Illinois.

Pola was born in Serbia. Her father was the Serbian ambassador to the US. She grew up in the Serbian embassy in Washington DC. She had an insatiable interest in politics, both national and international. When Annie had what she called her Hillary lunches, Pola was the one who lead the discussion. We ate with the Triandises many times. The conversation was always stimulating.

Another couple deserves special attention. Ray and Carol Smith are our neighbors down the hall. We see them every morning heading out the door to go to the pool in the courtyard behind the Grand Ave. building. Carol is wearing a bathing suit and a beach robe. She is in a wheelchair being pushed by Ray. There is a device that enables Carol to be lowered into the 85-degree water, enabling her to go through set of exercises prescribed by a physical therapist.

Ray sees to it that Carol goes to the dining room for dinner every evening. They go to all the happy hours. They attend the townhall meetings. We see them at most of the concerts. Ray is making it possible for Carol to live as normal a life as is possible given her limitations. Ray Smith is an outstanding example of what it means to be a devoted husband. I admire Carol for her courage and Ray for his devotion.

This might be a good time to talk about Jack and Valarie Cumming, two highly intelligent and well-educated people. He from Princeton, she from Brown. They were honored as volunteers of the year for 2019. A well-deserved honor it was.

Valerie goes about her business in a quiet and unassuming way. I have told how she volunteered to be the recording secretary for the Philanthropy committee.

In her working days Valerie developed exceptional skill in the use of the Microsoft Excel program for organizing and interpreting data. She became aware that the treasurer of the Residents Association was having difficulty in preparing the monthly report of financial activities. Valeria very quietly arranged to be copied on the source documents that came to the treasurer. She began running parallel with the treasurer and was able to correct mistakes before the report was complete. She continued to perform this service in her quiet way, until it was no longer needed.

Valerie has a green thumb. She takes pleasure by keeping the small garden patches around the Green Ave. Library. She is also a docent for the Flower Felds each spring.

Jack sponsors a study group each week entitled "Topics for Thinkers"

His major commitment is on a national level. He has a fervently held desire to secure the passage of national legislation that will prevent retirees from becoming the victims of incompetent owners/operators of retirement communities who declare bankruptcy, leaving the residents with no home, no service and no recourse.

Jack devotes a great deal of time, energy and money attending meetings of the National Continuing Care Residents Association. He is a director of this organization and is a regular contributor to their monthly newsletter.

Jack likes to kid me that his knowledge of George Fox is greater than mine. George Fox was the founder of the Quaker faith, known as the Society of Friends. I was raised as a Quaker. I attended Quaker schools.

There is no gossip to be shared about one other couple. They are just two genuinely nice people who came here as a married couple. I like to take credit for helping them make the decision to become residents at CBTS.

You may remember that I described my routine of a walk on the beach and how I rewarded myself with a stop at Starbucks.

I joined a small group of regulars who enjoyed their coffee, sitting together on the sidewalk in front of the store. Gail Walker was a retired teacher. Her husband, RD, had also been a teacher. RD had a good friend with whom he rode bikes several days a week. They surfed whenever possible. The friend's name was Bill Spore.

Bill was approaching the end of his career as an ob./gyn physician. He planned to retire when he was 60. Gail suggested that Bill should consider moving into CBTS. Gail knew how happy that Annie and I have been living there.

When I told Annie abut Bill and Gracie, she agreed that we should invite them for dinner. We did and as you might suspect it was a very pleasant experience. I could tell that Bill was persuaded. I assured him that he could continue with his activities. Gracie was not quite convinced. "You are not going to prison." I told Gracie. I told her that we had residents who continued with their career. Jackie Allen was still working a school nurse.

Bill and Gracie have become two of our most popular and loved couples.

Gracie has made a name for herself in a rather spectacular way. Give me a drum roll. Some background please.

La Cage

Early in our stay here at CBTS my attention was drawn to an activity that was going on in the long corridor on the first floor of the Main Building that runs from the Seashell to the employee's locker room.

Long tables had been covered with tablecloths. A variety of jewelry and some small clothing items were displayed. It was a thrift sale. The items came from residents who had died. These were items that remained in the apartment after their families removed everything they wanted. Beverly Gift had volunteered to be the manager of the thrift shop.

As the years progressed, the number of residents who died each year increased. More space was needed for the thrift shop.

One of the unappreciated benefits of living at CBTS is the two levels of parking in the Main Building. There are lot of unused parking places. Management agree to allow the thrift shop to set up in the Southeast corner of the lower level. Chain ink fences were installed to provide security for the merchandise. Furniture was now being offered for sale. A name was given to the activity. It was now called Le Cage. Beverly continued as the manager for several years.

Irish Killion was one of the most active and valuable volunteers in those early years. She had experience in a retail business where fine items were sold. She could appraise items that were contributed, giving them a price that would attract a buyer.

Beverly earned a well-deserved retirement. Irish was willing to take over as manager. She served for several years.

Gracie needed something to do while Bill was doing all his biking and surfing. She could see that volunteering to work in Le Cage would be worthwhile activity and something she would enjoy.

She was a natural. People love to work with her. Irish was slowing down. Without meaning to, Gracie began to take over the role that Irish was no longer fulfilling.

One of the jobs that the Le Cage volunteers perform is to visit the apartments of residents have died, after the families have taken everything that they wanted.

The former occupant of our apartment had lived there since the project opened. I was in the apartment the day the Le Cage crew came in to determine what they wanted. The family had been ruthless to find what they may have thought was a treasure that had been hidden away. There were clothes everywhere. The closets had been emptied. The bookshelves were over-turned. There was no furniture. There was nothing that would be of value for Le Cage.

On days when they do find large items that they believe will sell in Le Cage, they arrange with our maintenance department to have whatever brought down to Le Cage. Items that cannot or will not sell are donated to organizations like the Salvation Army.

The physical work that the Le Cage volunteers put forth is remarkable. Husbands with strong backs are called upon. A sense of pride has developed with the Le Cage volunteers.

Gracie's leadership skills and her enthusiasm for the mission have combined to produce outstanding results, month after month.

You may, or perhaps should ask, what happens to all the money that is generated from Le Cage. The Residents Association is charged with this responsibility.

A Board of Directors consisting of a president, vice president, treasurer, secretary and four members at large are elected to serve two-year terms. The elections are staggered to give some continuity to the Board.

A reserve fund of $50,000 was established to provide legal protection to the board members should their actions result in litigation.

The newly elected Board of Directors is taking a much more pro-active role in term of their obligation to put these funds to good use. I share Gracie's concern that there should be an on-going procedure as the funds will continue to be earned.

Gracie and Bill came into line behind me at the salad bar one evening. This was before the quarantine had been invoked because of the corona virus.

They each told me much they had enjoyed My Annie, the biography I wrote about my beloved wife. Gracie asked if I planned to write another book.

"Funny that you should ask, I have several pages written about what I am calling "Life in the Old Folks Home.""

Bill said he had a story that might be of interest. I could see a big smile on Graces' face. She was proud of her man and the story I was about to hear.

He was one of six octogenarians who formed a relay team

that set an international record for swimming the Catalina Channel.

I will deviate from Bill's story a moment to tell why the Catalina Channel attracts more interest than ether the Maui Channel from Lahaina to Lanai or the English Channel from England to France.

William Wrigley Jr. of chewing gum fame bought the island in 1920. He developed the town of Avalon as a resort desti-nation. Beginning in 1921 he brought the Chicago Cubs, the major league baseball team that he owned, to Catalina for spring training.

The island has been used as a site for making movies. One movie company brought 14 bison to the island and left them there. Today there are about 150 bison who roam the island.

Sometime in the 70's Wrigley deeded 80% of the island to the Catalina Island Conservancy. It will remain unchanged.

The town of Avalon is in a safe harbor that is surrounded by hills. Wrigley built a mansion on high on the East of the harbor.

Tourism is the only source of income. Consequently, the business that has been developed along the waterfront ca-ter to the wants and needs of tourists. Two restaurants, a couple of clothing stores and a few curio shops do a good business the two days a week when a cruise ship arrives.

The Catalina Channel has been a challenge for many ways of crossing it. Water skiers have been doing it for years, towed behind ever increasingly powerful boats. Paddle borders and kayakers are another group that cannot resist the challenge.

Bill's group of six octogenarian swimmers will be a first. He acknowledged that he would be the youngest member of the team, the only one who was not a master swimmer. It was his loyalty to his long-time friend that caused him to accept the invitation. Bill is such a quality guy that I am sure he never thought that his friend Dave had another thought in mind when he organized the event. He wanted his friend to have the experience of swimming in a master's event. Dave is highly regarded and would have no trouble getting four other master swimmers to join in the event. His endorsement of Bill was all that was needed to get the approval of the other swimmers.

Dave's confidence in his friends' ability was not misplaced. Bill completed his three swims in good time and his contribution to the event's success was acknowledged.

Bill Spore is one of several of our residents who has had an experience that separates them from the rest of us.

Rescue of Apollo 13

Don Harvey is another resident who has a truly remarkable experience

When the mission control people at Houston received the word about the explosion in the lunar module, they determined that Don was one of the people they needed to have with them when they communicated with the astronauts on board Apollo 13. I was impressed at how complete the records are that have anything to do with spacecraft and how they ae assembled.

Don was working in the science library at USC when he got a call from Joyce telling him to call his boss at TRW. He was wanted in Houston to assist in the recovery of the four astronauts.

Don had specific knowledge of the construction of the firewalls of the chambers in which the rockets were fired. Based on a model he had developed while working at TRW

When he got to Houston he was able to give assurance to

the engineers who were controlling what was on board the spacecraft, that their plan to use one of the other rockets to bring the module out of orbit, would not jeopardize the integrity of the module on a course back to Earth.

He knew the amount of fuel used by the burn of the rockets needed to bring the module out of orbit, would not affect the integrity of the module.

The people in charge moved forward using the rockets they needed, the module came out of orbit and a safe landing in the water north of New Zealand was accomplished.

Don said he had been awake for nearly three days. He was in a room with no windows and had no idea what time or what day it was.

Americans place astronauts high on the list of heroes, right up with sports stars, academy award winners and musical stars. The thought of losing the lives of three astronauts was unacceptable.

Don is entitled to be proud of is role in the rescue of Apollo 13.

The Savior of the Atomic Bomb

We must go back to 1942 to tell the story of the next outstanding resident. Glenn Quillen was born in 1917, during the height of World War I. He learned how to be a machinist in high school, in Berkeley, California. He demonstrated exceptional skills.

He had no difficulty getting hired after school. He married Signa, his high school sweetheart. An ad appeared in the Berkley newspaper offering a well-paid job to a highly trained machinist. The job included room and board. It was in Oak Ridge, Tennessee.

After Glenn established his ability by giving a demonstration at his workplace, a team of FBI agents interviewed him. He was being treated like a celebrity.

Once they arrived in Oak Ridge everything possible was done to make hem comfortable in their new home. His wife was offered a job, which she was grateful to have. They had told her that Glenn would be working long hours. All he knew was that this was a hush hush project and that it contributed to the war effort. Pearl Harbor had made a patriot out of every American

The FBI team made it clear to Glenn that everything he was going, to be doing, the people he would meet, and he work he was assigned was classified.

Here at CBTS, Glenn and Signa were living across the hall from our first apartment on the North corridor. Their door was left open much of the time. We could see that they lived an unconventional life. There were two microwave ovens. No furniture in the living room. It was filled with boxes.

Sigma told us that she drove into L.A. every day to collect the rents and check on the managers of their rental properties. Apparently, they did not eat together. That was why there were separate microwave ovens.

The last two paragraphs are pure gossip and have nothing to do with what made Glenn the outstanding man that he was.

Once the Quillen's got settled in their home in Tennessee, Glenn was introduced to Edward Teller, the nuclear physicist, who became known as the father of the H bomb.

Glenn worked with Teller for most of the next three years. He was machining parts in gold, a metal that is so soft it breaks apart easily. It took all of Glenn's significant skill to produce the results Teller was looking for.

The bomb was developed. With the courage of Harry Truman who gave the order, the Enola Gay dropped the first bomb on Hiroshima Japan. The war ended soon after. Glenn Quillen was an unsung hero. His skill was a contributor to the atomic bomb that may have saved the lives of untold numbers of American and Japanese servicemen, had the invasion of Japan been undertaken.

Glenn was a regular attender at Men's Breakfast while I was acting as the host. He would sit quietly, listening to all the "wisdom" that was being exchanged. Then he made a comment that was the only suggestion that made sense. I looked forward to what he had to say.

There is more about Glenn. On his 100th birthday, with the company of an instructor, he dove out of an airplane, at an altitude of 8,000 feet. On his 101st birthday he rode a zip line. He was looking for something to do on his 102nd birthday, but he did not make it.

Within a very few weeks of the end of his life, I received a call from Glenn asking me to come and visit him. He was propped in a hospital bed. I could I hardly recognize him.

His family filled the living room. We chatted for a few minutes and he thanked me for my friendship. I am so glad I made that visit. His friendship was one of my life's treasures.

Finale

February 20, 2019 was a black day in my life. Annie moved on to the next stage, whatever that may be. She was fortunate that she experienced no pain at the end. That big heart just quit. She was able to say good-by to two of our children. I was a patient in our skilled nursing facility and got the word from the director of nursing. She gave me a big hug and helped to ease the pain, pain that will never leave me.

Our children have surrounded me with the comfort that you knew they would. For the first two weeks they took turns spending all-day with me, so I was never alone. I continue to receive the comfort from our many friends here at CGTS, many of whom have suffered the loss of a spouse.

I have learned to be grateful for the sixty-nine years we had together. They were, for the most part, happy and exciting years. I will miss her every day of what is left for me. We were not only lovers; we were good friends. We shared everything.

As I go through my days, something will come up that I want

to share. I turn to tell her, but she is not there. This is what is hard.

The quarantine under which I am now living, has kept me in our apartment for the past several weeks. There is so much of Annie in this apartment. She took great pride and worked hard to make our home attractive, wherever that happened to be. The paintings in our bedroom and in the living, room were all her choice. We knew the artist who painted the two Hawaiian scenes.

One of her favorite pastimes was making collages. She would cut scenes and colors from her travel magazines which she put together to make a very attractive picture. There are three of them hanging in our apartment.

She was a collector. The china cabinet contains dozens of pitchers. There were too many in her collection too be displayed in the cabinet, so she arranged the overflow on a shelf above the cabinet. Central to these pitchers is a colorful Russian samovar

The corner cabinet is a story. Annie's father refinished it. He replaced the missing panes of glass in the door with glass that contained imperfections. He found the glass at his place of business. This cabinet contains more of Annie's treasures.

The seven girls who comprised the group in her nursing class who affiliated together, joined to give her a wedding present. It was a set of Fostoria crystal glasses. She was overwhelmed by their generosity. Annie was the first member of the group to get married. They had gotten to know me because I courted Annie throughout their training.

There is what is known as a tea set of Stangl pottery. It consists of a tea pot, six teacups and saucers, cream pitcher, and a sugar Thee are six medium sized plates. It is very colorful, with contrasting colors of purple and off-white.

The bottom part of the cabinet is solid wood. Her father might not have approved, it was where we kept our booze.

Annie will never leave me. As long as I live, and it may not be much longer, I keep her in my heart. It is because of what she gave me throughout the years we were together that I will be able to die a happy man.

CPSIA information can be obtained
at www.ICGtesting.com
Printed in the USA
BVHW041142030221
599288BV00015B/177

9 781977 229373